First Generation Gratitude

Gratitud a la Primera Generación

Written by
Diane Mylod Rodriguez

Illustrations by
Andrea Perusquía Mendoza

Editing & Design by
Moriah Mylod- Daggett

“The creation of a thousand forests is in one acorn.”

— Ralph Waldo Emerson

This book is dedicated to my mother and father; and to all lineages who took courage to leave their country to begin anew.

Este libro está dedicado a mis padres y a quienes han tenido el coraje de dejar su país para comenzar una nueva vida.

Thank you for being brave and leaving your country. It must have been scary to leave your home behind to live in a new country.

Gracias por dejar atrás a tu país y ser valiente. Seguramente tuviste miedo de dejar tu hogar para empezar en un país nuevo.

Thank you for all your childhood stories, traditions, and culture. I hope to share this unique way of life with all whom I share my life with.

Gracias por las historias de tu infancia, tus tradiciones y tu cultura. Espero poder compartir mis experiencias con los que convivo.

Thank you for working hard for us to give us what we needed. Your laborious work reminds me of all immigrants having hard work.

Gracias por tu ardua labor y darnos lo que necesitábamos . Tu trabajo siempre me hizo pensar en los migrantes que trabajan largas jornadas.

Thank you for the fun trips you took us on, no matter how big or small you may have believed them to be. The park and grocery store visits are some of my favorite memories.

Gracias por los divertidos viajes. No importaba qué tan costosos o sencillos eran. Las idas al parque y al mandado son de mis recuerdos favoritos.

Thanks for all the meals you cooked for the family. The flavor from our culture's cuisine reminds me of where we are from.

Gracias por los deliciosos platillos que cocinaste. La comida de nuestra cultura me recuerda de dónde somos.

Kkkk
nn-nn-nn

Thank you for bringing us joy with your sense of humor, even though it took some time to "get" your jokes, they bring a smile to my face today.

Gracias por tus intentos de hacerme reír, aunque tomó tiempo comprender tus bromas; recordarlas me hace sonreír.

pintos
ay como claveles morados
sufren

Thank you for making Sundays so special by singing your songs- while we watched you make meals from your upbringing.

Gracias por los Domingos maravillosos, mientras cantabas y cocinabas comidas de tu crianza

"Little beans I paint...purple carnations...Ay how they suffer the ones that are in love." -Linda Escobar

Thank you for attending Parent-Teacher Conferences and having trusted in me to take responsibility for my education.

Gracias por ir a las juntas con mis maestras y confiar en que yo fuera responsable por mi educación.

Thank you for being the life of the party with your enthusiastic singing and dancing. You have passed down the music of our culture to be sung and appreciated for future generations.

Gracias por ser el alma de la fiesta con tu canto y tu baile transmitiste la música de nuestra cultura.

Thank you for making me feel proud of who I am and inspiring me to continue our traditions. I will spread your enthusiasm, goodness, and love with others.

Gracias por hacerme sentir orgullosa de ser quien soy y por inspirarme para continuar nuestras tradiciones. Seguiré compartiendo tu entusiasmo y tu amor con los demás.

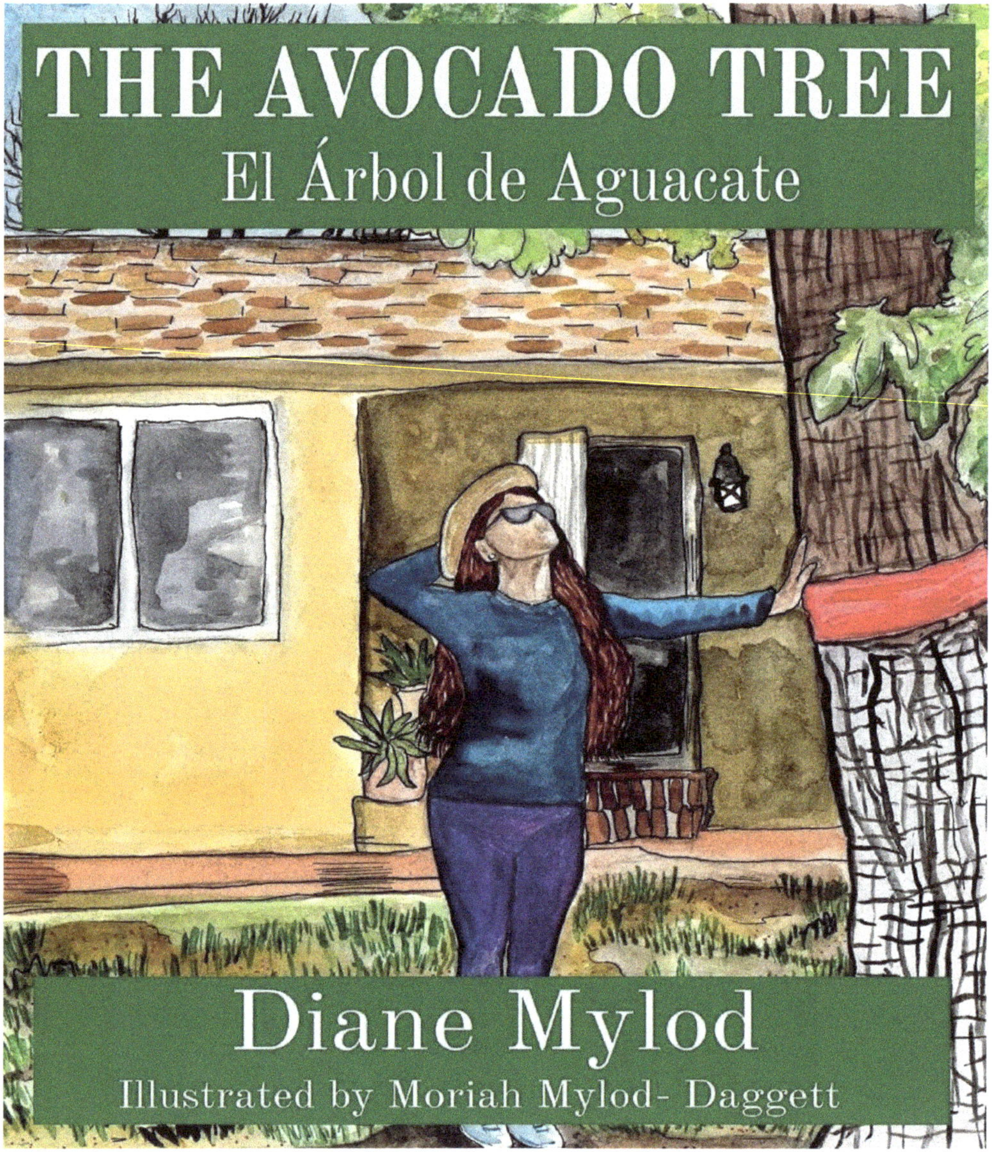
THE AVOCADO TREE
El Árbol de Aguacate
Diane Mylod
Illustrated by Moriah Mylod- Daggett

Thank you for planting fruits and vegetables in our yard. The Avocado tree you planted produces delicious fruit for all to enjoy.

Gracias por sembrar frutas y verduras en nuestro jardín. El Árbol de Aguacate que plantaste produce deliciosa fruta que seguimos disfrutando.

About the Author

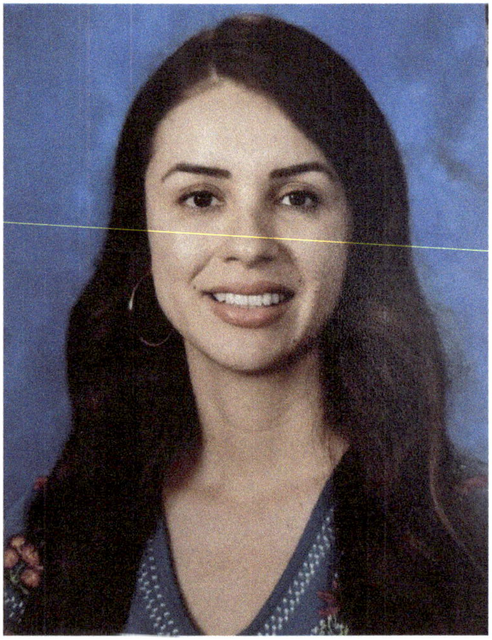

Diane Mylod, BA is a mother to 2 boys, Educator, and Author of the The Avocado Tree, a language immersive children's book about hope after grief. Diane is living in Phoenix, Arizona and was born and raised in Glendale, Arizona. She is an Arizona State University graduate, and elementary school teacher for over 10 years. Diane has experience with teaching in a refugee program where she worked with children who were refugees from Syria, Iraq, and Mexico in 2016. Diane has also taught children in a dual language academy that was a full immersion Spanish program. Diane wishes to continue to work with children in the public or charter education system for the state of Arizona. She is inspiring to continue to write children's books and work with immigrant children in the future to help those families in need.

About the Illustrator

Andrea was born in Queretaro, Mexico and migrated to the USA in 2006. Since she was little, she has always enjoyed daydreaming and making visual representations of her ideas, topics of interest, feelings or just things that bring joy. While living in Queretaro she studied Fine Arts and worked at the Art Museum of Queretaro planning workshops for visitors and working mostly with children. In the USA she completed a master's degree in education at ASU and has been teaching Art and Spanish to Elementary School Students. She has participated in several collective shows and some of her work belongs to the School of Transborder Studies at ASU, the Phoenix Children's Museum and Private Collectors.

About the Author and Illustrator

Diane and Andrea met in 2018 when Diane joined Andrea in teaching Spanish at a Dual Language Academy in the community they both live in. They both taught second graders Spanish in an immersion-rigorous program at a well-known public school in the state of Arizona. They quickly discovered they shared many things in common as Mexican women who are from the same age. They made a great team as public school teachers as well as established a supporting and caring friendship together. Andrea and Diane taught at that program for 3 years together and before leaving, Diane encouraged Andrea to pursue her passion for art and asked her to illustrate First Generation Gratitude. Andrea has also been the Spanish editor in both of Diane's published books and continue to have more plans for their future together in the art world.

Notes to caregivers & parents of children:

This book is another way to share your history with your children and children's children. As children of immigrant parents, we hold a deep gratitude for our ancestors in search for a better life.

A su vez es otra manera de compartir tu historia con tus hijos y ellos con los suyos. Como hijos de padres inmigrantes tenemos una profunda gratitud para nuestros ancestros; que buscaron una nueva vida.

About:

First Generation Gratitude is a multi-cultural children's book written in both the Spanish and English languages. This story celebrates the gratitude we have for our ancestral roots and for those who came to new countries before us. This story is for parents and caregivers who are proud of their heritage and who wish to keep the traditions and story-telling alive in the many ways that each culture expresses. It is through honoring our loved one's through art, culture and education that teaches children to be proud of where they come from-- and how the pride of our ancestor's story continues to be told from the heart of those who came after. This book is for anyone, and it is especially for all families who are immigrants or had previous generations of immigrant parents, grandparents and so on.

www.ingramcontent.com/pod-product-compliance
Ingram Content Group UK Ltd.
Pitfield, Milton Keynes, MK11 3LW, UK
UKHW060121010826
14089UKWH00006B/89

9 798218 087319